Battle of the Atlantic

When war was declared between Britain and Germany in 1939, Hitler decided to strike at Britain's weakest point – the convoys which brought oil, food and other essential supplies across the grey wastes of the Atlantic to the beleaguered island.

This book tells the story of those nerve-racking days between September 1939 and May 1943, when Allied merchantmen battled relentlessly against the superior German U-boats for mastery of the ocean routes. At first the conflict was dominated by the Germans. Their torpedoes and mines blew up millions of tons of British shipping, and thousands of lives were lost. Slowly the tide turned in favour of the British – radar and asdic were developed, ships, minesweepers and escort carriers were built in steadily increasing numbers. But, in the end, it was the selfless courage of the seamen, who continued to fight when all seemed lost, which really won the Battle of the Atlantic.

A WAYLAND SENTINEL BOOK

Battle of the Atlantic

Kenneth Allen

The Battle of the Atlantic was the dominating
factor throughout the war. Never for one
moment could we forget that everything
happening elsewhere, on land, at sea, or in the
air, depended ultimately on its outcome.
  Winston Churchill

WAYLAND PUBLISHERS LONDON

More Sentinel Books

The Story of Gunpowder   *Kenneth Allen*
Tourney and Joust   *Steven Jeffreys*
Nelson's Navy   *Roger Hart*
A Medieval Siege   *Steven Jeffreys*
War in the Trenches   *Matthew Holden*
Genghis Khan   *Michael Gibson*
The Legions of Rome   *Matthew Holden*
The Samurai of Japan   *Michael Gibson*
The French Foreign Legion   *Nigel Thomas*
The Wars of the Roses   *Kenneth Allen*
The Battle of Britain   *Anthony Hobbs*
The Crusades   *Matthew Holden*

Frontispiece : The sun sets on an escort of French destroyers.

SBN 85340 220 5

Copyright © 1973 by Wayland (Publishers) Limited
101 Grays Inn Road London WC1

Set in 'Monophoto' Baskerville and printed offset litho in
Great Britain by Page Bros (Norwich) Ltd, Norwich

Contents

List of Illustrations

1. Early days

Britain has long been separated from her neighbours by a defensive "moat" – the North Sea, English Channel and Atlantic Ocean. For centuries this moat has been Britain's greatest strength, and has helped defeat many threats of invasion. Yet, with the twentieth century, this strength became a source of danger. For Britain, a country of more than fifty million people, is primarily an industrial nation, sending her manufactured goods all over the world. In return there is a continual inflow of grain, meat, and other foodstuffs, fuel, and raw materials. Any threat to the merchantmen bringing these vital supplies is a threat to the whole nation. Without them, Britain's people – and factories – would starve.

This danger was acute in 1914 when World War One began. Britain's ocean life-lines were threatened by the vast German navy, her commerce by raiders, submarines and mines. The threat was even greater with the outbreak of World War Two in 1939. Not only had Britain's population increased, needing more food; but to the menace of destroyers and submarines was added that of bombers and torpedo-carrying aircraft, and more dangerous mines. Germany's navy could not compare with that of 1914, yet she had powerful "pocket" battleships better than any similar ships of the Royal Navy.

Hitler and Germany were determined to win this war, not by the clash of great fleets, but by all-out attacks on Britain and Allied merchantmen, especially in the Atlantic. If Germany could sink these ships faster than they could be replaced, Britain would have to surrender.

As Winston Churchill, Britain's great war leader stated: "The Battle of the Atlantic was the dominating factor throughout the war. Never for one moment could we forget that everything happening else-

Below Submarines were first used in World War One. Here, four crew members of an early German submarine scan the sea during a lull in the fighting (1917).

where, on land, at sea, or in the air, depended ultimately on its outcome." And again: "Dominating all our power to carry on the war, or even keep ourselves alive, lay our mastery of the ocean routes and the free approach and entry to our ports." On Sunday, 3rd September, 1939, war was declared. What was to become known as the Battle of the Atlantic had begun.

German ships take action

During August, 1939, two of Germany's three 10,000-ton pocket battleships slid quietly out of harbour and, under cover of darkness, headed out into the Atlantic. One was the *Graf Spee* bound for the South Atlantic. The other was her sister ship, the *Deutschland*, bound for the North Atlantic. With them went their supply ships, the *Altmark* and the *Westerwald*. By dawn, all four ships had disappeared into the vast emptiness of the ocean. This was not difficult to do: the Atlantic, stretching from the Bering Strait to the Weddell Sea, covers more than 31 million square miles.

Even as the grey German battleships steamed out of harbour, German U-boats were taking up their stations in the Atlantic. Their orders were to patrol the Western Approaches – the areas to the north-west and south-west of Britain. Most British-bound shipping had to pass through here. They had to lie in wait until they received the radio signal that war had been declared.

Preparations for war. *Above* A German torpedo boat (1936); and *below* after her launch H.M.S. *Prince of Wales* is towed away to be fitted with her "teeth."

Nor did Britain wait for the war to become official. On 26th August, 1939, the Admiralty flashed a signal to all 2,500 British merchant ships. Every one was ordered to leave its usual route and steer clear of any strange ship that might loom up over the horizon. Those bound for British ports were told to get there as quickly as possible. Some 110,000 tons of cargo were unloaded every day in Britain.

At the same time, the Admiralty assumed control of every British ship afloat, and began to organize the convoy system. Unfortunately, the British government had let the fleets run down since World War One, and despite an urgent building programme the Navy only expected to have 21 capital ships (battleships and carriers) by 1940 as against 68 in 1914, and 69 cruisers as against 103. Even so, the Royal Navy was to assume the command of the sea. From the moment war broke out, except for an occasional blockade runner, no German merchantmen sailed the seas.

First blood

The passenger liner *Athenia* was heading west across the Atlantic, bound for Montreal. She had sailed from Liverpool during the afternoon of the previous day, 2nd September, 1939, with 1,103 passengers and 315 crew. Because war seemed imminent, her captain had been ordered to change his normal route.

At 11.15 on the morning of 3rd September, Britain's Prime Minister, Neville Chamberlain, told the world by radio that Britain was at war with Germany. When a breathless radio operator arrived on the *Athenia*'s bridge with this startling news, the captain ordered full speed ahead. His crew hurried around the ship making sure that when darkness fell the liner would be "blacked out" and so invisible to any lurking submarine.

When the liner was some 250 miles north-west of Northern Ireland she was sighted by *U30*, a patrolling German submarine. Her captain, Lt. Cdr. Lemp, drew in his breath as he saw the bulk of the 15,000-ton liner looming up in his periscope. He, too, had been told that his country was at war with Britain, and believing the liner to be a troopship he did not hesitate. A few seconds later a torpedo was streaking towards its target. It struck, exploding with a great sheet of flame.

Passengers were trapped as the icy waters of the Atlantic thundered in. Many were drowned almost at once. A woman survivor said later: "I was standing on the upper deck when suddenly there was a terrible explosion, and I was thrown to the deck . . . When I recovered from the shock I saw several men lying dead on the deck near me. I was fortunate in getting into one of the lifeboats, but it was dreadful to see others in the water clinging to our lifeboat which was already too full to pick them up."

Below Anxious crowds look up at Big Ben as it strikes 11 a.m. on 3rd September, 1939 – the hour Britain's ultimatum to Germany expired. They know that war is at hand.

The liner sank fifteen hours later. 112 of her passengers, including some neutral Americans, lost their lives. The survivors were picked up by destroyers which had raced to the spot when the Admiralty heard the grim news. The *Athenia* was the first casualty in the Battle of the Atlantic, a battle that was to drag on for six years.

The convoy system

The Admiralty soon began to gather merchant ships together to sail under the protection of escorting warships. This convoy system was not a new idea. It was used centuries ago by the ancient Romans to bring their corn fleets through the pirate-infested waters of the Mediterranean.

During World War One, the first true convoy did not sail until the spring of 1917. But it proved so successful that, by June, 1917, all munition and food ships from North American ports were sailing in convoy. By July, 1917, all outward bound ships were doing the same.

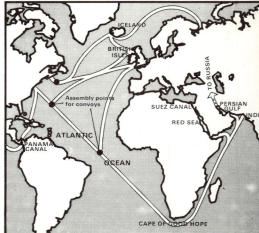

Convoys were organized to protect vital merchant shipping. *Above* The Atlantic convoy routes; *left* the formation of a daytime convoy; and *below* the speeds of the different convoy vessels.

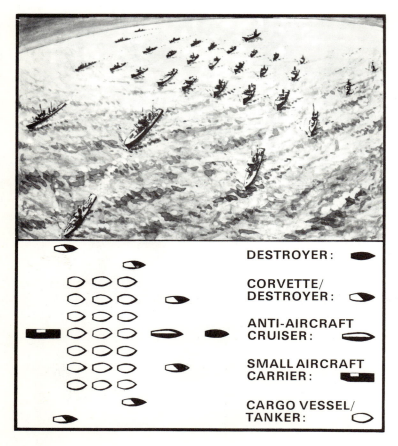

DESTROYER:

CORVETTE/
DESTROYER:

ANTI-AIRCRAFT
CRUISER:

SMALL AIRCRAFT
CARRIER:

CARGO VESSEL/
TANKER:

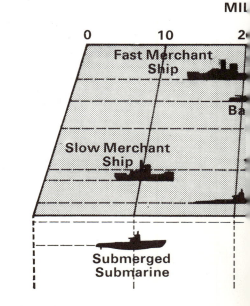

MIL

Fast Merchant Ship

Slow Merchant Ship

Submerged Submarine

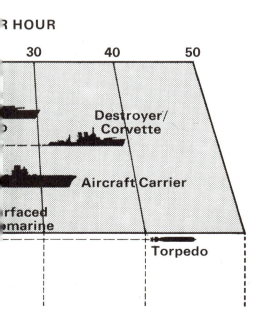

30   40   50

Destroyer/
Corvette

Aircraft Carrier

rfaced
marine

Torpedo

In World War Two, the first convoys left British ports on 7th September, 1939. For the next nine months, British merchant shipping was used to bring food and materials into the country, and to move men, guns and supplies across the Channel to France where Allied troops faced those of Germany. The fall of France and the evacuation of Dunkirk in June, 1940, virtually closed the North Sea and the English Channel to shipping. The only life-line left open was across the Atlantic.

Convoys proved the best form of protection, but they had their drawbacks too. They caused delay at the start of a voyage, for all the ships had to wait until the very last one was loaded. A convoy could not sail faster than its slowest ship, though separate convoys were arranged for fast and slow ships. There was much delay in unloading, too, as all the ships arrived in port together. This put a great strain on harbour facilities.

The size of a convoy varied. By 1943, the average number of ships was fifty, steaming in the shape of a rectangle, in columns of about ten ships. Cruisers, destroyers, corvettes, armed merchant cruisers and armed trawlers were all used as escorts. If there was any chance of attack from a surface raider, a battle ship or aircraft carrier usually joined the escort group.

The ideal warship for convoy protection was the destroyer, the Navy's maid-of-all work. Here again, there was an acute shortage. In 1939, there were only 216 destroyers and sloops available, with 33 more being built. Yet the volume of sea traffic to be protected was as great as ever.

The men of the Merchant Navy

Britain's life in World War Two depended on the men of the Merchant Navy, yet these men stubbornly remained "civilians," outside the Royal Navy. They worked for shipping companies and signed on for each voyage, often choosing their ship and where they would sail. After May, 1941, however, they became "reserved": they could not leave the sea for any other profession; they were guaranteed pay between voyages, and two days' leave for each month's service.

At the outbreak of war the Merchant Navy was greatly under strength, as its officers and seamen were called up for service in the Royal Navy. Most of them, about 12,000, were in the Royal Naval Reserve and served in merchant cruisers such as the *Rawalpindi* and *Jervis Bay*. Fortunately there was a large reservoir of manpower to call on. Between the two World Wars, British shipping had declined, and many officers and seamen were working ashore. In September, 1938, they were asked to volunteer if war broke out; a year later, nearly 13,000 men were immediately available for sea service.

The backbone of the Merchant Navy was the experienced and tough professional seaman. Many had been at sea since boyhood. Such men hated spit-and-polish. They wore what they liked aboard ship and, when ashore, could only be picked out from others by the small silver-coloured M.N. badge in the buttonhole of their shore-going jacket, when they remembered to wear it. In terms of manpower, the Merchant Navy was small compared to the Royal Navy, and rarely exceeded 120,000 men.

They kept Britain fed with at least one-third (by weight) of her food. They brought in the vital raw materials, and carried armies and materials to fight overseas. Without them Britain's army and air force

Below Britain's food supply depended on her Merchant Navy. At the outbreak of war, thousands of fishermen volunteered for service on the Atlantic convoys. Here, a group of trawler skippers are shown how to use a Lewis gun.

would have been powerless. For example, every four-engined bomber that flew to Germany from Britain needed 1,500 gallons of fuel oil. Some of the strikes on enemy territory involved 1,000 aircraft, needing $1\frac{1}{2}$ million gallons of oil. This could only be supplied by the ships – and the men of the Merchant Navy. This was what the Battle of the Atlantic was all about.

Loss of H.M.S. "Courageous"

At the outbreak of the war, Britain had three aircraft carriers in the Atlantic – the *Ark Royal*, *Hermes* and *Courageous*. The first of these was often reported sunk by the German radio, but not until November, 1941, did a torpedo finally send her to the bottom. Before then she had many narrow escapes. Her first was on 14th September, 1939. The *Ark Royal* was cruising off the Hebrides when she was sighted by Lt. Cdr. Clattes, Commander of *U39*. As the carrier's great bulk slid across the mirror of his periscope, he fired a salvo of torpedoes. For some reason they exploded too soon and the *Ark Royal* was undamaged. The explosions alerted the escorting destroyers. They dashed to the spot, forced the submarine to surface and took the crew prisoner.

But *U39* was soon to be avenged. Three days later a similar submarine, *U29,* sighted a dark outline on the horizon. Lt. Cdr. Schuhardt waited until it drew nearer. Then, to this great joy, he realized it was a large aircraft-carrier. It was the *Courageous,* part of a submarine-hunting group. Schuhardt waited, hardly daring to breathe as the ship drew nearer, and then – at the vital moment – the carrier turned so that the whole of her side presented him with a perfect target. Within seconds a salvo of three torpedoes hissed towards the ship. Without waiting to see the result, the U-boat crash-dived to avoid the destroyer escort. As the submarine plunged many fathoms down, it was suddenly shaken by three large explosions, and then several smaller ones. Schuhardt's torpedoes had all struck home. The *Courageous* was doomed.

A dramatic account of the sinking was given by 18-year old naval writer Hughes. "When we realized that we had been torpedoed," he said, "our men were so infuriated that they threw depth-charges

Below H.M.S. *Courageous*, one of Britain's three great aircraft carriers, which was sunk by a German U-boat in September, 1939. The 'planes were kept in the hangar under the deck, and raised by hydraulic lift to the flight deck for take-off.

overboard in an effort to sink the U-boat." But the *U29* managed to escape. On her return to base, Schuhardt found himself the hero of Germany. His little boat had sunk a British capital ship of 23,000 tons with the loss of 518 of its crew. It was the first such success made known to the German people. The German Admiralty had kept very quiet about the *U30* and the sinking of the *Athenia*.

Rescue by flying boat

Early in September, 1939, the *Kensington Court* was homeward bound from the Argentine with a cargo of wheat. She was a typical tramp steamer of 4,863 tons, salt-stained and scarred from her voyages around the world. As she entered British waters her look-out yelled in excitement. He had spotted a grey hump thrusting out of the water on the port side. It was a U-boat. Captain J. Schofield at once

The Sunderland, one of Britain's first flying "battleships." These flying boats were particularly useful for sea rescue work.

ordered an S.O.S. to be radioed out, and turned his ship's stern towards the enemy. At the same time her ancient engines began to pound violently, driving her through the water at a speed she had never reached before.

Suddenly there came a loud bang and a flash. The next moment a column of water shot skywards as a 3.5-inch shell exploded in the sea near her bows. The range rapidly closed, and when the fifth German shell struck the water only a few feet from the tramp's side, Schofield gave three blasts on her whistle – abandon ship.

In the hurry to get away, one of the three lifeboats capsized. Hardly had the other two picked up the survivors than a sixth shell struck the tramp amidships. There was a flash of flame, a dense cloud of greasy black smoke, and the ship began to settle in the water. As her crew sat watching at their oars, the gallant old ship slid slowly beneath the waves. The U-boat, too, disappeared.

The men began to row. Hours later, one of them looked up – and gave a cheer. Coming in low towards them was an aircraft bearing the familiar British roundels. Their S.O.S. had been received. To their surprise, the aircraft circled them once then gently settled on the sea, rising up and down with the motion of the waves. A few minutes later another of the strange flying-boats appeared and skimmed to the surface near the other. Captain Schofield said later: "While we were getting on board a third plane came over and flew around. We wondered how they would get us on board, because the sea was choppy, but a door in the side of the flying-boat opened and a small collapsible boat was pushed out. It was the modern method of rescue and we had never had any experience like it." Neither had anyone else.

A new type of mine

On 18th November, 1939, the Dutch ship *Simon Bolivar* was struck and sunk by a mine. The mine was quite unlike those of World War One which exploded when a passing ship struck them. This new weapon was a "magnetic" mine. German aircraft were dropping hundreds of them by parachute around Britain's coast.

Four days later a magnetic mine was dropped from a seaplane near Shoeburyness, a small town at the mouth of the River Thames, and fell into the mud. Some soldiers went out to inspect the metal monster and, realizing it was "different," reported the find to the Admiralty.

Before dawn next day, a party of experts from the *Vernon*, the torpedo school at Portsmouth, arrived to examine the mine. They soon realized that it was of a new magnetic type. Making sure that they had no metal about them, some experts carefully took paper rubbings of the nuts, bolts and other fittings on the outside of the mine. From these, special tools were made to render the deadly weapon harmless.

Lt. Cdr. John Ouvry volunteered to dismantle the mine. He worked alone, but kept shouting to the rest of the party stationed some distance away, to say what he was doing, in case he was suddenly blown up. Ouvry removed one detonator, only to find another. Ten anxious minutes ticked past before he had made the mine safe. It was then taken by lorry to Portsmouth for further inspection. Ouvry was later awarded the D.S.O. (Distinguished Service Order) for his courage and skill.

Magnetic mines worked on a simple principle. When being built in the shipyard, a ship becomes charged with magnetism. At sea, it becomes a kind of floating magnet. When a ship passes over a magnetic mine moored below the surface, it attracts

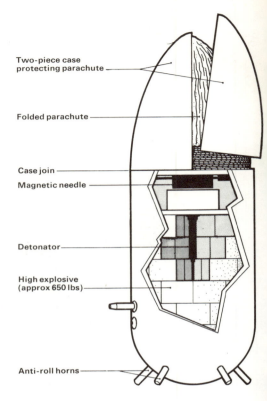

Above A diagram of a magnetic mine. In five days in November, 1939, fifteen British ships were destroyed by such mines.

Above An early German
magnetic mine recovered near
the Thames estuary in 1939.
The rule has been put
alongside to show its height.

a needle in the mine upwards towards it. This needle touches off a detonator and the mine explodes beneath the ship's bottom. Between 18th and 22nd November, 1939, fifteen ships were lost in this way.

The solution was to neutralize the ship's magnetism by "de-gaussing," wrapping wire cables round the ship's hull to absorb the magnetism. At one time, 1,200 *miles* of wire cable were being used every week in order to neutralize vessels.

2. The ocean raiders

A year before war broke out, Adolf Hitler, Germany's ruler, had to choose between two plans. Either he could use all Germany's naval resources to build a huge fleet of submarines, minelayers and other vessels to attack merchantmen and destroy the enemy's seaborne trade. Or else – Plan Z – he must build a battle fleet bigger than that of any other power. This would take time, but his experts claimed that war would not begin for at least ten years. Hitler agreed, and chose Plan Z. But to Hitler's surprise, his invasion of Poland on 1st September, 1939, made Britain declare war on Germany two days later, long before Plan Z could be completed.

At this time, Germany had two battleships, the *Scharnhorst* and the *Gneisenau*. Two more, the powerful *Bismarck* and *Tirpitz*, were nearly completed. Germany also had three 10,000-ton "pocket battleships" – the *Admiral Scheer*, the *Deutschland* (later renamed *Lützow*) and the *Graf Spee*, as well as nine well-armed cruisers, and scores of armed merchantships.

The British Commonwealth had a fleet of twelve battleships, some of them quite old, three battlecruisers and six aircraft carriers. There were also fifteen 8-inch gun cruisers, twenty-six smaller cruisers and more than a hundred destroyers. Curiously, she had nearly as many submarines as Germany, forty-nine in all.

Because Hitler had chosen Plan Z, Germany had only fifty-seven U-boats available for service. These boats could not all be at sea together. Some were on training missions, others were being repaired or else refuelled and resupplied in harbour. Nevertheless,

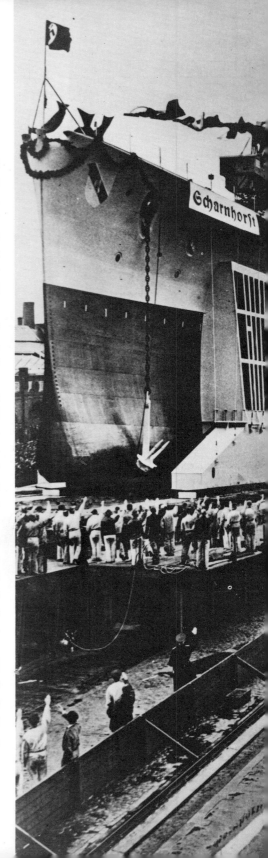

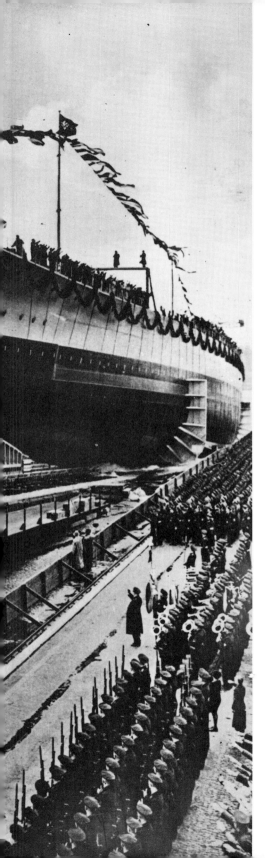

before war began, twenty-one U-boats were at sea, stationed on the main routes to Britain.

At first, the greatest threat to Allied shipping seemed to be the *Graf Spee* and *Deutschland*. But Hitler refused to allow the two battleships to attack. He still hoped, having dealt with Poland, to make an early peace with the Western powers.

By 26th September, it was clear that Britain and her allies were prepared to fight. Yielding to pressure, Hitler at last ordered the *Graf Spee* and *Deutschland* to destroy every merchant ship in their respective areas.

Left The launching of the German battleship *Scharnhorst* in 1936. Notice how the spectators are giving the straight-arm "Heil Hitler" salute. Although the ship is being launched, it is in fact only the keel that is complete. The ship will have to be taken to another part of the shipyards to have the superstructure built on.

A most gallant action

In 1939, the Admiralty took over several liners and turned them into armed merchant cruisers. Unlike the other ships of the Merchant Navy, which were armed with a small gun at the stern just for defensive purposes, these armed cruisers were designed to play an offensive role as auxiliary warships. But their largest guns were only 6-inch calibre. It was not much to challenge the massive guns of enemy warships.

One of these ships was the 16,000-ton liner *Rawalpindi*. She was cruising to the south-east of

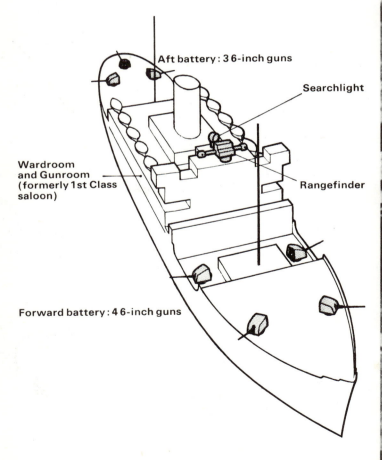

Aft battery: 3 6-inch guns

Searchlight

Wardroom and Gunroom (formerly 1st Class saloon)

Rangefinder

Forward battery: 4 6-inch guns

Iceland when, at 3.30 p.m. on 23rd November, 1939, an enemy ship was sighted. It was the *Scharnhorst*, a battleship of 26,000 tons and armed with nine 11-inch and twelve 5.9-inch guns. Although his own ship carried only 6-inch guns, Captain Kennedy did not hesitate. He sent his crew to action stations and changed course so that the enemy was brought onto his starboard quarter. Soon afterwards another warship was sighted. This was the *Gneisenau*, sister ship to the *Scharnhorst*. The odds were now formidable indeed.

At 3.45 p.m., the *Scharnhorst* fired a salvo from her 11-inch guns at a range of 10,000 yards. The *Rawalpindi* replied with her four starboard guns. A second German salvo fell short, but the third struck the British liner, putting out all her lights. As the ship reeled under the impact, a fourth salvo screamed through the air and demolished her bridge and radio room.

Despite the terrific concentration of fire from both ships, the *Rawalpindi* gallantly kept on firing until every one of her guns was knocked out, and huge flames were leaping skyward from fires raging amidships. After forty minutes of this unequal combat, the battleships ceased firing, and the three boats from the *Rawalpindi* which were not shattered by shell-fire were lowered. Two of them, containing more than thirty men, were picked up by one of the German ships. Those in the other boat would have been picked up too, but a British cruiser was seen approaching. By then the Germans had had enough, and slipped away into the rain and darkness.

Far left Diagram of an armed merchant cruiser – a liner converted into a temporary warship. But they were no match for mighty German battleships like the *Scharnhorst* and the *Gneisenau (left)*.

Raider at large!

For nearly three months, an unknown German raider had been preying on merchantmen in the South Atlantic and Indian Oceans. She was known to be a fast pocket battleship that could easily outrun any British battleship that sighted her. But any cruiser fast enough to catch her would be crushed by her superior gun power.

This was the problem facing Commodore Henry Harwood, with his force of three cruisers, the *Exeter*, *Ajax* and *Achilles*. On the morning of 15th December, 1939, the *Exeter* sighted smoke on the horizon. She signalled: "I think she is a pocket-battleship!" Quickly, the *Exeter* turned west, while the lighter *Ajax* and *Achilles* raced on a north-easterly course, to engage the enemy from different angles. This would force her either to divide her fire power or ignore one of the cruisers.

The raider was identified as the *Graf Spee*. She opened fire at long range with her 11-inch guns, firing at all three cruisers at the same time. At first they could not reply, but the range shortened as they raced towards her. When the *Exeter*'s 8-inch guns began to belch smoke and flame, all the *Graf Spee*'s turrets swung round to deal with her. Very soon German shells were hammering the *Exeter*, destroying one of her turrets, wrecking the wheel house, and killing or wounding nearly everyone on the bridge.

But the 6-inch guns of the *Ajax* and *Achilles* now opened up, and the German had to re-engage them. Within half an hour of the first shell being fired, the *Graf Spee* seemed to have had enough. Dense black smoke began to hide her sleek outline and she turned away, heading west. The three cruisers followed, at a safe distance of fifteen miles.

The badly injured *Exeter* was ordered to the Falkland Islands. The others, despite shell damage,

Above H.M.S. *Exeter,* one of the three British cruisers that hunted down the German pocket battleship *Graf Spee.*

clung to their quarry until it slunk into the safety of the neutral River Plate, in South America. Commodore Harwood, in the *Ajax*, signalled to the British Minister ashore, asking him to do all he could to delay the raider's sailing to gain time for reinforcements to arrive. With their huge opponent at anchor off Montevideo, the two small cruisers settled down to await the dawn. . .

Right Naval ratings examine the damage done to H.M.S. *Exeter* during her encounter with the *Graf Spee*.

War of nerves

Hans Langsdorff, Captain of the *Graf Spee,* was a worried man. He had brought his ship into the safety of Montevideo where he could have the battle damage repaired. But he could not stay long, for every day would bring British reinforcements closer. Under International Law, any merchant ship clearing a neutral port has to be given twenty-four hours start over an enemy warship leaving the same port. So, to stop the *Graf Spee* sailing, the British authorities ordered their merchant ships to sail at the rate of one a day!

At dusk on Sunday, 18th December, 1939, the *Graf Spee* steamed slowly out of Montevideo harbour. Her battle flags were flying and, fully repaired, she was once more a powerful fighting machine. Following in her wake was a German merchantman, the *Tacoma.* As the *Graf Spee* headed for the open sea, the Uruguayan coastline was thronged with sight-seers. It seemed that a battle between naval giants would be fought within sight of the shore.

Then, as the sun set, the watchers were startled by an enormous flash, followed by the dull boom of a heavy explosion. More explosions followed – the *Graf Spee* was ablaze from stem to stern. Soon afterwards the British warships that had been expecting a desperate battle moved slowly and in silence past the flaming wreck of the once proud battleship.

Captain Langsdorff was no longer aboard. He had set explosives about his ship, opened her sea cocks to the Atlantic Ocean, and ferried a skeleton crew across to the *Tacoma* which then took them to Buenos Aires. The following night, he spread the old ensign of the

30

Imperial German Navy on his bedroom floor and shot himself.

The *Graf Spee* had sunk only nine Allied merchantmen totalling 50,000 tons, a poor result for such effort. Her sister ship, the *Deutschland*, had been even less successful. She had sunk only two ships of a total tonnage of less than 8,000 when she was recalled to Germany on 1st December, 1939. So far the notorious pocket battleships had not come up to expectations!

Left Two photographs showing the end of the *Graf Spee*. Rather than risk capture in battle, Captain Langsdorff preferred to scuttle his own ship.

Heroic fight of the "Jervis Bay"

During October, 1940, the third Germany pocket battleship, the *Admiral Scheer,* slipped undetected into the Atlantic and began to hunt for victims. On 5th November, she sighted the merchantman *Mopan* which she sank after taking off the crew. Even as her lifeboats were being swung back into place, her look-out yelled in excitement. Looming over the horizon was a forest of masts. It marked the arrival of a large convoy, HX-84, homeward bound from Halifax, Nova Scotia.

More and more masts began to appear until 37 ships, of all types and sizes, were seen. They had only one escort, the 14,000-ton armed merchant cruiser, *Jervis Bay.* Captain Fegen, commander of the *Jervis Bay,* at once saw the grave threat to his convoy – with her speed and powerful guns, the *Scheer* could easily sink them all. Yet there was hope. Dusk was falling, and Fegen knew that in the darkness many of his ships could escape. He signalled to the convoy to disperse, then turned his bows towards the oncoming raider.

The *Scheer* immediately opened fire with all her 11-inch guns. The captain of one of the merchantmen said later: "We made our escape as quickly as we could, but we owed that escape mainly to the gallantry of the *Jervis Bay.* She went right out to meet the German challenge, although everyone knew what her fate would be. Her crew were facing almost certain death but, despite that, they maintained the highest tradition of British seamen. The *Jervis Bay* immediately came under fire from the German raider. The encounter was of short duration. A few sharp salvoes caught her and she went on fire. All the time she kept replying with her guns, but these were no match for the powerfully armed battleship. Soon all was over. The *Jervis Bay* was

Below Alert on board an armed merchant cruiser. One man keeps a look-out for raiders, while the other signals to the convoy they are protecting: "Danger at hand!"

ablaze, and her guns ceased firing.''

It took the *Scheer* nearly three hours to finish off her opponent. By that time night had fallen, and the convoy had scattered. In consequence, the *Scheer* was able to locate and sink only five of the 37 vessels, then had to leave the area in haste, since British warships were racing to the scene to avenge their gallant comrade.

The epic of the "San Demetrio"

One ship in the convoy escorted by the *Jervis Bay* was a large new oil tanker, the *San Demetrio*. Although she had scattered with the rest, she was still within range of the *Scheer* when the *Jervis Bay* was sunk. A salvo of shells struck her, and the order was given to abandon ship. As the crew pulled away in the boats, the tanker burst into flames which showed bright against the dark night sky.

As dawn broke next day, sixteen tired and wet men in one of the tanker's boats stared out over an empty sea. A ship was sighted later, but passed without noticing them. In the afternoon another was seen. She had obviously been abandoned. As they drew nearer they realized that it was their own tanker, the *San Demetrio*. She was in a terrible state. Fires were still blazing and water was sweeping across her decks. As night was approaching Second Officer Arthur Hawkins, in command of the boat, decided to wait until morning. When dawn broke the sea was empty once more – the *San Demetrio* had disappeared.

The men hoisted a sail and after some hours sighted the tanker again. They closed with her, and although she was still burning they climbed aboard and began to fight the fires. Working desperately, they managed to get the hoses into operation and pumped out the engine room.

At last the fires were all put out. But how could they get the ship home? The engines were working, but there was no radio, charts or compasses, and only a half-burned auxiliary steering wheel aft. This was patched up and, steering by the stars, they began the hazardous passage home. They went slowly, for the ship was down by the bows and the seas continually swept over the crumpled and buckled decks. Ireland was sighted on 13th Nov-

Above November, 1940. Survivors of a torpedoed ship are picked up by a destroyer in the bleak Atlantic.

Right In the early days of the war, small and lightly-armed escort vessels were all that could be spared to protect the convoys.

ember, and as the water was too deep to anchor, Mr. Hawkins kept the tanker circling until dawn.

On 16th November, the charred and battered tanker reached the safety of the Clyde after one of the most dramatic voyages of the war. Salvage money of more than £14,000 was paid to the survivors and to a stoker, John Boyle, who had died during the passage. Despite broken ribs and other injuries, he had carried on for three days in the engine room.

Sink the Bismarck!

By mid-1941, the Atlantic convoys had had a terrible battering. Things were so bad that the War Cabinet decided not to issue any more details of the tonnage lost. The figures were too depressing! Then, on 21st May, 1941, the Admiralty received stunning news. The *Bismarck*, the world's greatest battleship, in company with the heavy cruiser *Prinz Eugen*, had left harbour and was somewhere at sea.

Admiral Sir John Tovey acted swiftly, well knowing what damage the mighty *Bismarck* could do to the vital Atlantic convoys. He issued one curt order – "Sink the *Bismarck*!"

There were five exits from the North Sea into the Atlantic. Tovey had to ensure that each one was guarded, although he guessed that the enemy would try and slip through the Denmark Strait between Iceland and Greenland. Two cruisers, the *Norfolk* and *Suffolk*, were patrolling these waters, and were warned to keep a lookout for the German warships. Meanwhile, the *Hood* and *Prince of Wales* were sent racing towards Iceland.

Squalls of snow and sleet made observation very difficult but, on the morning of 23rd May, the cruisers sighted the enemy and managed to keep in contact throughout the long stormy night. Early next morning, the two cruisers joined them and, at first light, Vice-Admiral Holland in the *Hood* gave the order to open fire. Soon the four larger ships – the *Norfolk* and *Suffolk* were still out of range – were exchanging broadsides. It was seen that the *Bismarck* had received several hits. Then came disaster. A shell struck the *Hood*'s magazine and the 42,000 ton cruiser erupted in a sudden explosion of flame and smoke. Within minutes she was gone, taking all but three of her crew of 1,500 with her.

The *Bismarck,* also damaged, turned south and

Above The launching of the *Bismarck*, the most powerful of all the German battleships, on 14th February, 1939.

Left The British Admiral Sir John Tovey, who led the hunt for the *Bismarck*.

the *Norfolk* and *Suffolk* went on shadowing her. The *Prince of Wales* was damaged by seven direct hits, but still managed to fire several salvoes at the retreating enemy. Visibility grew worse. During the afternoon of 25th May, the British ships lost sight of their quarry. Next day, however, a Coastal Command aircraft sighted the battleship 550 miles west of Land's End, and radioed her position. There would be vengeance for the *Hood*.

The kill

On the morning of 26th May, 1941, it seemed as if the *Bismarck* would escape after all. The *King George V* and *Rodney* were too far behind to catch her, and the *Victorious* and *Prince of Wales* were heading for Iceland to refuel.

One hope remained. Somehow the German battleship had to be slowed down so that her pursuers could come within range. Fortunately the

Below The end of the hunt. German survivors rescued from the *Bismarck* are brought ashore at a British port.

Ark Royal was near enough to fly off a force of Swordfish torpedo bombers. Despite fierce anti-aircraft fire, the Swordfish pressed home their attack and scored two hits with their torpedoes. One struck the *Bismarck* amidships, the other aft. The latter damaged her steering gear and propellers, and the battleship was seen to make two complete circles before resuming course. Most important of all, her speed dropped to eight knots.

About 11 p.m., Captain Vian and four destroyers came racing out of the darkness, and both the *Maori* and *Cossack* scored hits with torpedoes, slowing the *Bismarck* down still further. The long night passed. Early on the morning of 27th May, the *Norfolk* sighted the long sleek outline of the German battleship through the mist and driving rain. She dashed off the message – "Enemy in sight, twelve miles to the south of me" – to the *King George V* and *Rodney*. Soon these two ships sighted the enemy themselves.

Within minutes, the 16-inch guns of the *Rodney* and the newer 14-inch guns of the *King George V* opened fire. The *Bismarck*'s guns replied but she did not score any hits. But she was being ripped and torn by the great shells that were exploding deep inside her. The end was inevitable and near. The *Bismarck* was blazing fiercely, and some of the crew were seen leaping from her flaming decks into the sea. Still she fought on, her battle ensign streaming out in defiance as the *Dorsetshire* closed and fired a salvo of torpedoes. Three struck her black flame-scorched hull. She listed to port, then rolled over to float upside down for a while. Then her bows tilted skywards and she slid beneath the waves. The *Dorsetshire* and a destroyer picked up 110 survivors, but reports of U-boats nearby forced them to stop this work of mercy.

Naval gunnery

In a large warship, the guns are controlled from the Director Control Tower. Details of range, speed and direction are sent to the gunlayers via the Transmitting Station (or T.S.). This T.S. is the nerve centre of the guns, and is always placed well below deck. It has a network of voice-pipes and telephones connecting it to the control tower and the guns. The guns are loaded and ranged onto the target and, when the director gunner is satisfied, he presses a master trigger which fires all the guns at once.

When a warship fires a salvo or number of shells together, the distance between the farthest and the nearest shots is called the "spread." The splashes made by the shells striking the water serve as guides for the observers. Some of the splashes from large shells can reach a height of 200 feet, and are easily spotted. If they are to the left or right, then the control officer has to correct the fall of shot. When he is getting a "straddle" – splashes in line with his own ship both over and short of the enemy vessel – he knows he is on target.

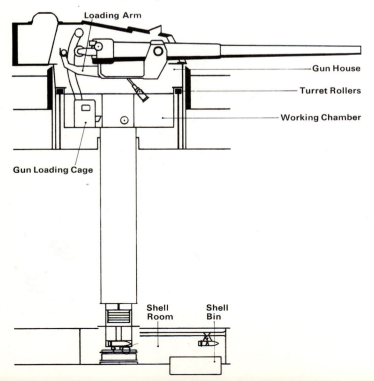

Above A naval gun crew go aboard a convoy ship, bringing their ammunition with them.

Left A cross-section of a 15-inch gun turret. The shells are raised from the shell room by power-operated hoists.

Sometimes he sees nothing at all. This may mean a direct hit. When the *Hood* was fighting the *Bismarck*, her early shooting was excellent. The first two salvoes were close, the third straddled her opponent. The *Bismarck* and *Prince Eugen* both fired in reply and the latter scored a hit within a minute. In the second action the *Bismarck's* main fire control was destroyed early in the battle and she did not register one hit.

Merchant ships were armed, too, usually with an old four-inch gun bolted onto a platform at the stern. When war began, no one foresaw the danger from aircraft attack, and a strange collection of weapons were put into merchant ships. These included a device which fired a wire into the air in the hope it would snarl an enemy aircraft's wings or propeller! Fortunately, better weapons later became available, such as the Bofors and Oerlikon anti-aircraft guns. Most of the gun crews in the Merchant Navy were merchant seamen who had taken a short gunnery course. Although they were civilians and amateur gunners, they were to sink several U-boats and shoot down many enemy aircraft before the war ended.

3. The U-boat war

The loss of the *Athenia* on the first day of the war led many British people to believe that ships would be sunk in their hundreds by the German U-boats. At first this was not so. By the end of 1939, losses caused by U-boats totalled 114 ships. But 79 ships had been scuttled by enemy mines, mainly of the magnetic type.

During this time the Royal Navy had lost, by torpedoes, the *Royal Oak,* the *Courageous,* an armed merchant cruiser, three destroyers and a submarine. The *Royal Oak* was sunk by a brave U-boat commander, Günther Prien. On the night of 13th October, 1939, he took his boat into the well-guarded waters of Scapa Flow, Britain's naval base in the Orkneys, and torpedoed the huge battleship with the loss of 24 officers and 809 men.

Thanks to the convoy system, U-boats did not at first do the damage that had been expected. Only four out of the 114 merchantmen lost had been in convoy; the others had been sailing alone. The

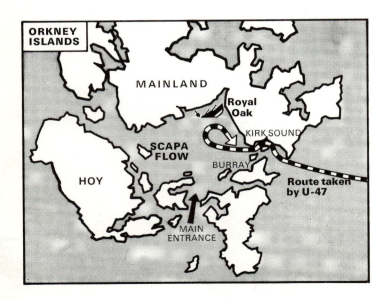

magnetic mine had been mastered and the pocket battleships chased off the seas.

The great weakness of the convoys was the shortage of long-range escorts. This shortage became even more acute in the spring of 1940. The campaign in Norway, and the evacuation of Allied troops from the Continent, took many warships away from escort duty. In addition, the massive German victories in Europe changed the whole pattern of U-boat warfare. Admiral Doenitz now had a string of ports from Norway to the Bay of Biscay. Strongly fortified bases were built on the French Atlantic coast at Brest, Lorient, St. Nazaire, La Rochelle and Bordeaux. The U-boats were now 450 miles nearer their stations in the Atlantic and this reduction in travelling time meant that more boats were available. They could also patrol further west, into the middle of the Atlantic, to reach an area outside the range of many escorts.

Then Britain herself was threatened by invasion. Many destroyers and sloops needed by the convoys were held in British ports ready to combat this new threat. The battles of the convoys – on which the outcome of the war depended – were about to begin.

Opposite Scapa Flow, Britain's naval base in the Orkneys. Here, on the night of 13th October, 1939, a U-boat managed to get through the defences and sink the battleship *Royal Oak*.

Below Admiral Doenitz, commander of the German submarine forces, welcomes a U-boat crew on their return from a successful tour of duty in the North Atlantic (1939).

Das Unterseeboot

Das Unterseeboot, or U-boat, is like other submarines – basically a long steel cylinder divided into compartments. The hull was designed to withstand great pressures of water. Attached to it were the ballast tanks which, when flooded with water, caused the boat to sink. As long as its engines were kept running it could be forced down below the surface where its position was "trimmed" by horizontal rudders, or hydroplanes. When it wished to surface, compressed air was blown into the main ballast tanks. This expelled the water, making the craft more buoyant until it rose to the surface. U-boats had two means of propulsion. On the surface, they were driven by two powerful diesel engines. Submerged, they switched to electric motors run off storage batteries which, unlike the diesels, did not need air. After

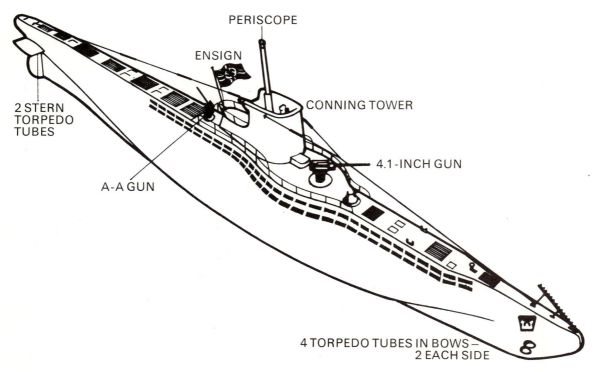

PERISCOPE

ENSIGN

CONNING TOWER

2 STERN TORPEDO TUBES

A-A GUN

4.1-INCH GUN

4 TORPEDO TUBES IN BOWS –
2 EACH SIDE

Above Inside a German U-boat. Hanging on the right is one of the twelve torpedoes it carried.

Left Diagram of a German ocean-going U-boat. The guns on the deck were for use against other ships and aircraft when the submarine had surfaced.

about twenty-four hours the batteries had to be recharged, and the U-boat was forced to surface. The diesels were used as generators. A typical U-boat was of 770 tons, 220 feet long, and had a cruising range of 9,000 miles. It was armed with the main weapon of all U-boats – the torpedo. U-boats also carried a naval gun for surface firing and, later, anti-aircraft guns as well.

U-boat crews, like all submariners, were hand-picked volunteers. Most ocean-going craft had a complement of forty-four officers and men. They lived amid a maze of cables and dials, pipes and gauges, in an atmosphere of fuel oil and stale food, foul air and sweat. They had to work as a team, able to get along with each other, and with great confidence in their captain.

When a U-boat went into action, the captain alone could see what was happening. He had his eye to the periscope – for the few seconds it was allowed to break surface – and no one else could see what was going on outside. The rest could hear the dull thump as their torpedoes struck the target. They could also hear the drumming of the hunter's propellers overhead as, silent and helpless, their bodies stiff with cold and strain, they waited while depth charges exploded around them, knowing that each moment might be their last.

Dark days

By the end of the first year of the Battle of the Atlantic, it was plain that Germany was winning.

The main reason for this success was that U-boat commanders had found a way to beat the "asdic." This was a device used to detect submerged vessels, and which the Allies had hoped would bring about a U-boat's destruction before it could attack. To combat the asdic, the U-boats stayed submerged during daylight hours, following a convoy by the sound of its throbbing propellers and an occasional peep through the periscope. They would only surface at night. The asdic was ineffective against a surfaced U-boat, and this allowed the boat to close with the convoy without being picked up. Also, its low superstructure was almost impossible for look-outs to spot. On the other hand, to the U-boat commander, the merchant ships were clearly outlined as black shapes against the sky, providing perfect targets.

Below The tonnage of Allied shipping sunk by U-boats *alone*, to the end of 1940.

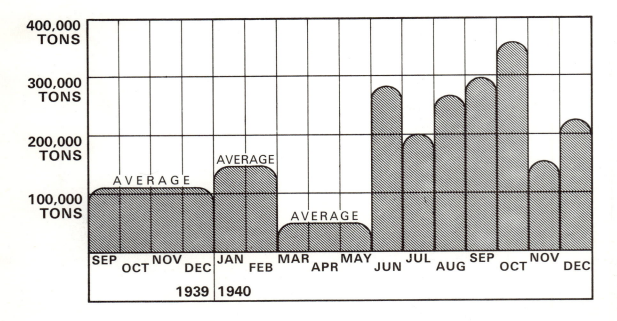

Sharp pulses of sound sent out by the search vessel echo back from any large submerged object to receivers on board. The time the sound takes to return tells the asdic operators how far away the object is

In fully developed asdic, three 'shapes' of pulse-beam are used to pin-point an enemy submarine:

1 Diffuse cone for general search

2 Broad, flat beam for finding depth of target

3 Narrow, vertical beam for finding bearing of target

Above How the submarine detecting device – asdic – works.
Below April 1940 – an Atlantic convoy outlined against the sky – a perfect target for any lurking U-boat.

On the surface a submarine could use its diesel engine, and make more speed than most of the convoy's escort vessels. Soon the confident U-boat commanders were slipping into the very heart of the convoy, where their torpedoes could hardly miss.

Before an attack, the merchantmen would be steaming quietly along, fully darkened, only a faint gleam from the binnacle lighting the face of the helmsman as he peered at his compass. Then suddenly there would come a roar as a torpedo struck home and bright flames speared into the dark sky. As the alarm bells jangled, and officers and men raced to their stations on bridge, engine-room or gun platform, there would come another explosion, and another.

The escorts would rush in, trying to get a "fix" with their asdics, and the water would erupt as depth charges exploded in their wake. This activity could last for most of the night as the convoy steamed on. Dawn would show a sea littered with charred debris and, here and there, the bodies of drowned seamen floating in their life jackets, white faces staring blindly at the lightening sky.

The wolf packs

On 11th August, 1940, Hitler announced that there would be a total blockade of the British Isles. All neutral shipping would be sunk on sight. This was a warning, and also a sign that Germany was staking everything on her U-boats winning the Battle of the Atlantic. Admiral Doenitz declared: "The U-boat will always be the backbone of warfare against England, and of political pressure on her."

Doenitz, who had been a submariner himself during World War One, then began a new plan of attack. Until the mid-1940s, U-boats had operated singly. He now began *Rudeltaktik* – or wolf-pack operations – using groups of up to twenty U-boats. He sent these wolf-packs out into the Atlantic to lie in wait, spread out at intervals along the Western Approaches. If a lone ship came into view, a U-boat could attack it. If a convoy was sighted, however, the boat had to report direct to Doenitz at his head-quarters, so that a whole pack could be brought in for the kill.

They would attack at night, emptying their torpedo tubes at the merchantmen, and then diving hastily to escape ramming or depth charges. By dawn, the weary escorts had usually given up the chase and the pack would settle down to follow the convoy until night came once more. Then they would start all over again, attacking and running night after night until the battered convoy finally reached port.

There seemed no answer to these tactics, for there were never enough escorts. About four U-boats were sunk each month, but this was not good enough. German shipyards could more than keep pace with these losses. On the other hand, about the same number of allied merchantmen were being sunk every day – more than six times as fast as they could

Below In their rather cramped quarters, the officers and crew of a German U-boat relax for a meal before continuing the hunt for Allied ships and convoys.

be built. In one year, nearly 100,000 tons of shipping were lost for each U-boat destroyed. The continual slaughter of the merchant ships was frightening. One homeward bound convoy, the SC-7, was attacked by seven U-boats, and lost seventeen ships in one night. HX-79, a convoy of 49 ships fell foul of Günther Prien. His *U47* and five other U-boats sank another fourteen. Winston Churchill wrote afterwards: "The only thing that ever frightened me during the war was the U-boat peril."

The deadly torpedo

The modern torpedo was invented in 1866 by an Englishman, Robert Whitehead, who was employed by the Austrian Government. But Austria did not appreciate the value of this new and deadly weapon, and Whitehead returned to England to work for the Admiralty.

The standard 21-inch torpedo used in World War Two contained 500 lbs. of high explosive packed in its nose. The rest of the long slim tube held the driving and steering mechanism, and buoyancy spaces.

At first the engines were driven by compressed air. But this left a tell-tale wake of white bubbles, so later the compressed air was replaced by an electric motor.

Earlier torpedoes exploded on striking the target. This was caused by a "pistol," a piece of steel projecting through the nose. On impact, the pistol was pushed back onto the detonating charge. Around this pistol was a device rather like a tiny propeller. As the torpedo sped through the water the propeller revolved, and only when it had completed enough revolutions could the pistol be forced in. This was to stop a premature explosion when the torpedo was fired.

Many torpedoes were faulty. Some ran too deep and passed under the target. Others struck but failed to explode. Günther Prien once fired a salvo of torpedoes at a seemingly solid wall of ships. Not

Below A cross-section of a late model torpedo.

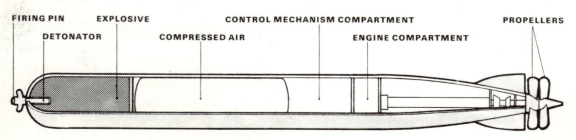

FIRING PIN   EXPLOSIVE   CONTROL MECHANISM COMPARTMENT   PROPELLERS

DETONATOR   COMPRESSED AIR   ENGINE COMPARTMENT

one exploded. At a second attempt, the same thing happened. Three days later a tempting target came into his periscope sights – the 31,000-ton battleship *Warspite*. Prien crept in close and at almost point blank range fired two torpedoes. Neither struck, but one exploded at the end of its run, alerting the escorting destroyers who came racing to the spot where Prien had crash-dived. He was severely depth-charged for a long time before he finally escaped.

The answer to these problems was the acoustic torpedo that "homed" onto the sound of a ship's propellers. The final torpedo of the war was a German invention known as the *Lut*. After it had completed a straight run the *Lut* would steer a predetermined zigzag course. But, by that time, most U-boats were being sunk before they had time to fire.

Below Firing practice with torpedoes was very necessary. Here a used practice torpedo is hauled aboard a Royal Navy ship for re-use.

Nerve centre

As soon as war began, the Admiralty set up a central point from which the movement of convoys and, later, the attacks on U-boats could be organized. In the large Operations Room, one wall was filled by a map of the North Atlantic. It showed the position of every convoy, outward or homeward bound, and the strength of its escorts. Each convoy was distinguished by letters showing the port from which it

Below Up-to-the-minute information about the position of Allied and enemy ships was vital. On board a cruiser, information from the Admiralty is plotted on charts.

had sailed, such as HX for Halifax, followed by a number – HX-5, and so on. This map was kept up-to-the-minute by Wrens who moved counters and numbered flags as fresh signals were received by the duty officer.

There was also a U-boat Tracking Room which passed on information to the Operations Room. This warned the Admiral commanding the Western Approaches when a convoy was in danger of attack. He could then warn the escorts to expect trouble, and also send additional warships – if they were available – to the danger area.

The Submarine Tracking Room and the Trade Plot, as the convoy map was called, were manned night and day. Information about the movement of U-boats came from many different sources. The most important were the radio direction finding stations, whose operators listened for U-boats using their radio. Warships too listened for radio signals. More were picked up when the wolf-pack tactics began – when a convoy was sighted, the U-boat had to radio the information back to Doenitz. Agents in enemy countries also passed on valuable news about the arrival and sailing of U-boats and other warships. And there were reports of actual sightings of U-boats by aircraft and surface vessels.

All this information was channelled through to the Tracking Room. Here the position of the U-boat in relation to the nearest convoy would be worked out and shown on the map. Urgent orders would go out to the convoy commander urging a change of course that would take him out of the danger zone. In the early days of the Battle of the Atlantic, there were many tragic moments in the Operations Room when the map showed U-boat packs converging on the convoys. The people on duty knew that there were often no escorts available to help them.

Three U-boat aces

Among the outstanding U-boat aces were three commanders – Otto Kretschmer, Günther Prien and Joachim Schepke. Each sank more than a quarter of a million tons of shipping. Curiously, their activities all ended within two weeks of each other during March, 1941. Prien, in *U47*, was shadowing an outward bound convoy when he was sighted by the destroyer *Wolverine*. The destroyer raced to the spot where Prien had crash-dived, and dropped a pattern of depth-charges. Badly damaged, the U-boat stayed down until dark, then surfaced once more. But the *Wolverine* was still waiting and this time her depth-charges brought oil and debris rising from the depths. Paying tribute to a gallant commander Admiral Doenitz said: "The hero of Scapa Flow has made his last patrol. We of the U-boat service proudly mourn and salute him and his men . . ."

Nine days after the destruction of *U47*, the boats of Kretschmer and Schepke, *U99* and *U100*, joined in an attack on the homeward bound convoy HX-112. It had been sighted by Lemp, whose *U30* had sunk the *Athenia* sixteen months before. The pack gathered, eagerly awaiting the chance to attack a large convoy of fifty heavily-laden freighters and tankers. For once the escort was a strong one – five destroyers and two corvettes. The odds seemed to be fairly even until three destroyers dashed off to tackle *U100* some miles away, and the other U-boat commanders slipped into the centre of the convoy. Soon the darkness was lit by the dazzling gleam of rockets and flares and the red glow of explosions and blazing ships.

Success came to the hard-pressed escorts when the white flash of *U100*'s wake was sighted by the *Walker*. The arrival of this destroyer sent the U-boat crash-diving, but although there was an intense bombardment from depth-charges, it survived and even surfaced later to continue the attack. This time, though, it surfaced too near the *Vance*, which tore down upon it, rammed it and sank it almost immediately.

Only a few of the crew were rescued. Even as they were being hauled on board the *Vance*, yet another U-boat was sighted nearby. The *Walker* was on hand to engage the newcomer, and after a brisk exchange of gunfire the U-boat disappeared, leaving a handful of her crew desperately swimming. The last to be rescued was the captain – Otto Kretschmer himself. Now that Prien and Schepke (who had been lost in *U100*) had gone, he was the sole survivor of a courageous trio of aces.

Below Captain Günther Prien, one of the most successful German U-boat commanders, is greeted by Admiral Doenitz on completion of yet another mission.

Strange capture

To the four-man crew of a Hudson bomber of Coastal Command, this patrol one morning in September, 1941, was just routine. Their plane droned over the rough white-capped waters of the Atlantic, which seemed empty for miles. Suddenly there was an excited shout from the navigator: "There's one in front of you!"

The pilot looked down. About 1,000 yards away, lying on the surface of the tumbling water, was the unmistakable sleek outline of a U-boat. The Hudson quickly dived, then climbed away steeply as its bomb whistled towards its target. The pilot brought the plane down low, its machine guns chattering as it swept across the U-boat. Then, as it turned to make another run, the submarine's hatch opened and a dozen men tumbled out on deck. But another run by the plane sent them all fighting to get back to the conning tower. The Hudson roared over the boat several times, her three machine guns blazing away. Then one of the U-boat's crew held up a white shirt and waved it to and fro, before draping it over the side of the conning tower. The submarine had surrendered.

While the Hudson was circling around the boat, it radioed the amazing news back to base and asked for help. Some hours later a Catalina aircraft appeared and the Hudson's pilot, fearing it might try and sink the prize, sent an urgent signal, "Look after our, repeat *our* submarine, which has shown the white flag." Then, after the crew had taken a final look at their capture, he set course for home.

The Catalina began to circle, her guns trained on the submarine. She kept this up all day, only breaking off her vigil when darkness fell. Daylight brought yet another Catalina to the scene. By then other ships were in the area. The crew of the

Below The crew of a captured German U-boat line the deck as the submarine is brought into Weymouth Harbour.

U-boat were taken off, and its bows pointed towards England. From that moment, for the next forty hours, Coastal Command aircraft were flying overhead, keeping a close and jealous watch over their capture, despite darkness and continual storms. In England, eager technicians descended on the U-boat to examine it in detail. This was the first time that a land plane had ever forced a submarine to surrender.

4. Battle for the sea lanes

Allied shipping losses for 1941 had been crippling. German U-boats, aircraft, raiders and mines had sunk 1,299 ships, a total of 4,328,558 tons. British shipyards could never replace this. A mere 87 U-boats had been destroyed, and German shipyards were keeping pace with these losses. Almost all their activities were now concerned with the building of new and better submarines.

The convoys were still desperately short of escorts. At times it seemed as if U-boats could attack them as and when they liked. In the late summer of 1940, however, help was promised by America. President Roosevelt agreed that fifty old but reconditioned

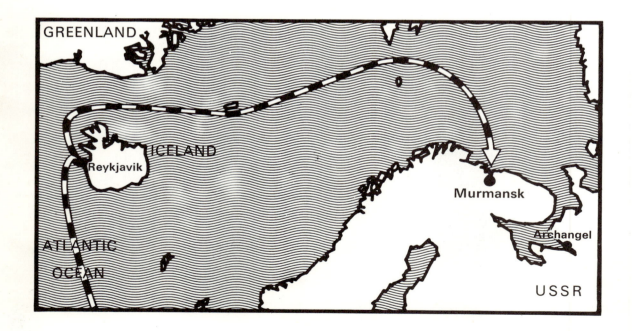

Above Constant vigilance was essential if the convoy was to get through safely. Here a raider is sighted, and the call for action stations goes out.
Left The route of the convoys to Murmansk, one of the most dangerous of all the convoy runs undertaken by the British in World War Two.

destroyers would be leased to Britain in exchange for bases in Bermuda and the West Indies. It would be some time, however, before these destroyers would be ready to go into action by the side of British warships.

In June, 1941, Hitler's armies stormed into Russia. For a time, they won victory after victory. Russia lost tons of precious war material – guns, tanks and shells – and called on Britain, her new ally, to help replace them. British convoys – designated PQ – had to sail north into the Arctic, to Archangel and Murmansk. Cruisers, destroyers and even battleships would have to go with them, weakening still further the vital Atlantic convoys.

In the spring of 1941, the C.A.M. (Catapult Aircraft Merchantmen) came into operation. Merchant ships were equipped with catapults which launched fighter aircraft, often Sea Hurricanes, when the convoy was threatened by enemy bombers. The first success came on 3rd August, 1941, when a Fleet Air Arm pilot shot down a Focke-Wulf after nine minutes. As it was impossible to land the fighter planes back on the ship, the pilots had to "ditch" in the sea, and hope to be picked up.

The desperate year of 1941 was coming to an end. 1942 would see the battle for the sea lanes – and for survival – reach its climax.

Off the American coast

In August, 1941, Winston Churchill and President Roosevelt met in Placentia Bay, Newfoundland. The two leaders pledged their countries to fight for a just peace. This declaration was known as the Atlantic Charter. The Battle of the Atlantic was discussed, too, and Roosevelt said that the American navy would do all it could to stop U-boats attacking Allied shipping west of Ireland. This would be a

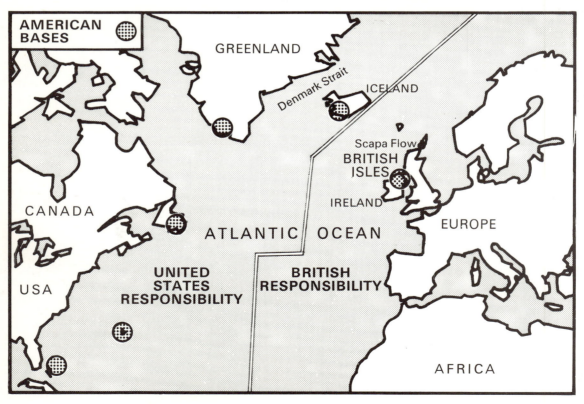

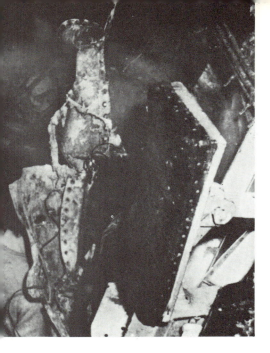

Above The torn and twisted metal on board U.S.S. *Kearney* shows where a German torpedo struck home.
Opposite The 1941 Atlantic Charter eased the task of Britain's Navy – the Americans promised to help protect Allied shipping west of Ireland.

great help to Britain's hard-pressed navy. It would free escort vessels for duty in the Eastern Atlantic where the wolf-packs were causing huge losses.

By October, 1941, American warships were on escort duty in the Western Atlantic. But U-boats were still attacking the convoys, and sank several ships. Then on 16th October, the *Kearney*, an American destroyer, was hit by a German torpedo. She managed to limp into harbour for repairs but, two weeks later, the American *Reuben James* was sunk 600 miles west of Iceland. The United States was technically still at peace with Germany.

On 7th December, 1941, the situation suddenly changed. Japan treacherously bombed the U.S. base at Pearl Harbor and America immediately declared war upon her. On 11th December, Hitler declared war against the United States. This began one of the worst periods in the entire U-boat war. Doenitz sent five crack submarines across the Atlantic to prey on American shipping. For months American merchantmen were being picked off at will. At first they were not even blacked out, but sailed with all lights blazing as if inviting a torpedo. Even when ships were blacked out, towns along the coast still glared with neon and other lights, against which vessels stood out in black relief. Radio operators also chatted unguardedly to each other, and valuable information was picked up by the U-boats. As a jubilant Doenitz put it: "Our submarines are operating close inshore along the coast of the United States of America, so that bathers and sometimes entire coastal cities are witnesses to that drama of war." However, by July, 1942, the convoy system was beginning to reduce the losses.

The Black Gap

In the early months of the war, many convoys left Britain under the protection of one or two armed trawlers only. After three days or so, the trawlers would signal "Good luck" and turn for home, leaving the convoy to sail on unescorted. There were just not enough "long-legged" escorts available for the whole passage. At the beginning of 1940, there was a gap of about 1,700 miles which had to be crossed by convoys without escorts. Not until June, 1941, did the first convoy cross the Atlantic with surface escorts all the way.

By the end of 1941, Britain began using long-range aircraft for convoy protection. Yet this only cut the gap by a little, for these planes could only operate a few hundred miles from base. Their presence, except in home waters, was merely a nuisance to the U-boats, who moved further out into the central Atlantic where they could operate free from both surface and air attacks. At first they

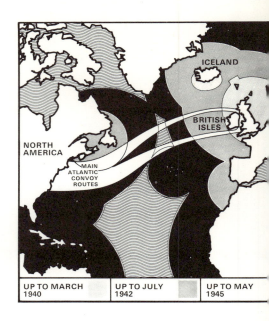

Above The gradual closing-up of the mid-Atlantic Black Gap.

found this a rich hunting ground – there were many ships sailing alone in the area. Later the convoys were better escorted, but by then the wolf-pack system of attack had been introduced, and the Black Gap, as it was called, became the scene of many bitter battles.

By July, 1942, new U-boats were leaving German shipyards at the rate of thirty a month, and this increased strength encouraged Doenitz to send a large proportion of his force into the Gap. He had lines of U-boats covering its limits so that they knew the moment a convoy moved into it. As more aircraft with longer ranges came into operation, the danger area gradually shrunk, especially when four-engined bombers began regular patrols from bases in North America, Greenland, Iceland, and Northern Ireland.

The main coverage, however, came from auxiliary carriers. After the C.A.M.s came the M.A.C.s (Merchant Aircraft Carriers). The first of these was a captured German freighter the *Hanover*, renamed *Empire Audacity*. She had a flight deck built on her from which fighter aircraft could take off and land without using the one-way catapult. German pilots were amazed when fighter planes suddenly appeared in mid-ocean, until they realized that they came from the *Empire Audacity*. From that moment U-boats made every attempt to sink her and, in December, 1941, they finally succeeded. But it was such ships and planes which finally closed the Gap.

Opposite An enemy bomber is sighted, and the gun crew swing into action.

The great raid

Early in 1942, grave news reached the Admiralty. The new German battleship *Tirpitz* was almost ready for sea. She was the most powerful warship in the world and would be able to do vast damage to any Atlantic convoy, no matter how strongly escorted. But there was only one dock big enough to take her – the U-boat base at St. Nazaire in France.

During March 1942, it was decided to attack St. Nazaire and make it useless both to the *Tirpitz* and to U-boats. "Operation Chariot" was headed by an American lease-lend destroyer renamed the *Cambeltown*, commanded by Lt. Cdr. S. H. Beattie. With her went a force of motor launches carrying 250 Commandos under Colonel Newman. Commander Ryder was in overall command of the naval forces.

The *Cambeltown* arrived in the River Loire on the night of 27th March, 1942, and slipped within 1,000 yards of the docks before the German shore batteries opened fire. The destroyer's old engines drove her on at full speed until she rammed the lock gates and stuck fast. Just before the impact, Beattie fired two torpedoes into the gates. They had delayed

action fuses which would not operate until similar fuses detonated the three tons of high explosive packed into the *Cambeltown*'s bows. Newman and his Commandos battled their way ashore and were soon blowing up vital lock machinery. By then, however, the German garrison had been alerted and furious fighting broke out. Despite a terrible crossfire, seven of the original flotilla of twenty-five launches managed to reach the open sea. Even though they were safe, the few survivors were discouraged – they felt sure that the attack had failed. There had been no great explosion, and it seemed that the fuses in the *Cambeltown* were faulty.

Next morning a large party of German technicians and officers boarded the *Cambeltown* to discuss how she could best be prized free of the lock gates. As they began their tour, the tons of high explosive blew up. Nearly all of the men were killed, and the lock gates which could have sheltered the *Tirpitz* lay in ruins. The raid was a triumphant success after all, and five men received the Victoria Cross – a record for one operation.

Above Colonel Newman, leader of Operation Chariot, the daring commando raid against the St. Nazaire dockyard, takes the salute during a parade in 1945. *Left* The German battleship *Tirpitz*, once the most powerful in the world. It was to prevent her using the French U-boat base at St. Nazaire that Operation Chariot was launched.

Fighting merchantmen

In 1941, naval and military gunners were posted to merchant ships to help man their growing armaments. Until then, the old 4-inch gun in the stern and maybe a Lewis machine gun on the bridge had been manned by merchant seamen as part of their other duties. The first success of these "amateurs" was gained when the war was only six weeks old. An old tramp steamer, the *Rockpool*, was fired on by a U-boat, but then brought her own gun to bear and forced her opponent to submerge. Soon the U-boat resurfaced, and the duel began again. For more than an hour, both vessels fired at each other without scoring a direct hit. But near misses had so damaged the U-boat that she could no longer dive and was sunk by a destroyer that had come to the *Rockpool*'s aid.

An even longer battle was fought between another tramp, the *Hopestar,* and a U-boat off Land's End. After the first torpedo, the tramp steered a crazy zig-zag course, firing at the submarine each time she sighted her periscope. Two more torpedoes were fired, one missing by only two yards. This strange encounter lasted from noon until dusk, when darkness and damage to her hull forced the U-boat to retire.

Another typical fight took place in the middle of a hard-pressed convoy. The *Cromarty* was changing course to avoid a torpedoed tanker ahead of her, when a U-boat was sighted. The merchant seamen gunners fired seven rounds, two of them hits. As her Captain, J. T. Hair, said later: "The submarine was seen to disappear stern first, her bows coming up as she sank. During the fighting my vessel hit something along the starboard side. In all probability we hit the submarine that had torpedoed the tanker . . ."

Below The terrible conditions in the Atlantic were only one of the hazards to be faced by convoy crews.

A thrilling duel took place a month later, in October, 1941. The *Lady Shirley*, a small trawler, was on patrol when she sighted a U-boat. Both vessels opened fire. Machine-gun bullets killed some of the Germans who were manning the U-boat gun, while their machine guns killed the *Lady Shirley*'s gun-layer. He was at once replaced and several hits were scored on the U-boat. Suddenly the men on its deck threw up their hands in surrender – a few moments later the U-boat sank.

Ships in convoy

By 1942, convoys had become larger. Many of them had fifty or more ships, and the task of getting them all to sea was tremendous. The commander was often a retired naval captain, brought back into the service as a Commodore. The convoy captains met with him to receive their sailing orders. These gave details of each ship's number in convoy, the speed, the distance to be kept between ships, the zig-zag course to be steered, and so on. The commodore warned them of the dangers of straggling, reminding them that "the safety of the convoy as a whole must come first."

The Commodore went on board his ship, a fast freighter, with a small staff of signallers – most of his orders at sea were given by hoisting flags, or flashing an Aldis signal lamp. Last minute prepara-

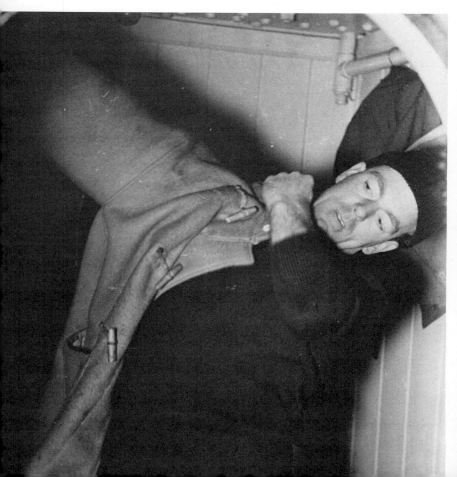

tions were made. Hatches and derricks were tightly secured, and each ship was completely blacked out. Darkened covers called "deadlights" were dropped over the portholes at night. The doors had a trigger device to cut off the light in the cabin when they were opened.

Sailing time arrived at last, and the ships left harbour to meet up with the other ships in the convoy. Shepherded by the escort vessels, the whole convoy put to sea – perhaps an old ship, caked with the salt of many oceans and flying the Greek flag; a smart Norwegian tanker; a small liner flying the red, white and blue stripes of Holland; and British freighters with their red ensigns. As the ships headed out on the first stage of their long passage, every officer and man knew that, before him, lay 3,000 miles of ocean where U-boats, Focke-Wulfs and surface raiders might be waiting. And that was not all. Nature could be equally dangerous – fog, storms and ice claimed many victims too. But come what might, the convoys had to get through.

Left The captain and officer of an escort vessel keep watch over the ships in their convoy. *Far left* Whatever the conditions "up top," routine has to go on. A crew member gets ready to go on watch.

Death of a liner

Early in October, 1942, the British Eighth Army in Egypt was ready to strike at Rommel's forces in North Africa. The British strength had been built up through Egypt by a steady stream of merchantmen. Among the ships were eight large passenger liners, turned into troopships.

The newest of these, the 23,000-ton *Orcades*, had already put her troops ashore, and with 1,600 passengers and a cargo of foodstuffs was homeward bound. She left Cape Town on 9th October, having been warned that a U-boat was lurking in the South Atlantic. After a night of rain and a rising sea, daylight found her on a southerly course at full speed.

Mid-morning boat drill was held. While some of the passengers were still removing their lifejackets, the great ship suddenly shuddered under the impact of a torpedo. Amid the strident clanging of alarms, there were two more explosions. The *Orcades* had been struck three times! The first torpedo had damaged propellers and steering gear, the others had struck forward, ripping great holes in the ship's side. Yet the engine room was undamaged, and the forward watertight bulkheads were holding. Captain C. Fox had already radioed an S.O.S., but he knew that it would be hours before help arrived. And the U-boat was still lurking nearby.

Fox decided to send the ship's boats away but to keep fifty volunteers on board to take the crippled ship back to Cape Town. Unfortunately, the last boat capsized and thirty-eight passengers were drowned. The rest of the boats were taken in tow by two motor launches and soon disappeared in the direction of Cape Town. The crippled *Orcades* slowly followed. The hours passed. Then, more than five hours after the first explosions, there came three more. The gallant liner had taken six torpedoes

Below General Montgomery takes the salute after the Allied victory at El Alamein – a victory in which merchant troopships and the doomed liner *Orcades* had played a significant part.

altogether! This time it was the end. The fifty volunteers had scarcely got clear in their lifeboats before the great liner heeled over onto her starboard side and slowly sank out of sight.

Three weeks later, the troops that she had landed helped smash Rommel's defences at El Alamein and, by 6th November, the victory in the desert was complete. The *Orcades* had not fallen in vain.

5. The tide of battle turns

The shipping losses for 1941 had been terrible, but 1942 proved even worse. Some 1,700 ships were lost, nearly 8 million tons, of which U-boats alone sank more than 6 million tons. Yet Admiral Doenitz was still not satisfied. Mainly because of the new type of "Liberty" ship being produced in American yards, Allied ships were for the first time being launched almost as fast as his U-boats could sink them. And Doenitz was losing submarines at a steady rate.

At last, by the end of 1942, Britain's long-awaited convoy escort ships began to appear. Many had been ordered in 1940 and were now ready for sea. In addition to invaluable destroyers, a new type of anti-submarine vessel was becoming available for

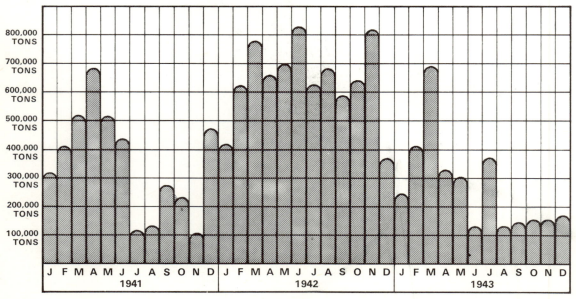

Above Land-based, long-range bombers like the Wellington provided much needed protection for the merchant convoys, but did not come into operation until the end of 1942. You can see what a difference they made from the table *(left)* of the tonnage of merchant shipping sunk by the Germans, 1941–43.

convoy duty. This was the frigate – a small ship, but fast and well-armed, and able to withstand the great winter storms that raged across the Atlantic.

Their arrival heralded a new pattern of convoy warfare. Until then, the Navy had too few ships to hunt U-boats to the death. Their main task had been to stay with the convoy at all times. Now, the arrival of the frigates meant an additional force which could play an offensive role. Their task was to leave the convoy, if necessary, and work as a striking force to hunt down the attackers. While one frigate tracked the U-boat with its asdics or the new radar, others would race in with depth charges and "pattern" the area with them.

The first of these groups began operating towards the end of September, 1942, but their effect was not fully felt until the following year. By then anti-submarine support groups had been formed. These were groups of six or seven ships – destroyers, frigates, and often an aircraft carrier with flight crews highly skilled in hunting U-boats. These groups did no escort duty, but merely stood by ready to help any convoy that was being attacked.

By the beginning of 1943, complete shore-to-shore air cover was being provided by the escort carriers, and by land-based British, American and Canadian bombers. At last the tide of the Atlantic battle was beginning to turn.

Mines and minesweeping

From the outset of the war, one great danger was mines. They were of two types: contact and non-contact. A contact mine was moored by a wire which kept it floating just below the surface. It was globe-shaped, and had several horns projecting from it which – when struck by the hull of a ship – caused the charge to explode. Non-contact mines included magnetic, acoustic and pressure mines. They did not have to be struck to explode. The first was exploded by the magnetism which exists in all ships; the second by the sound vibrations of a ship's propellers, the third by the downward water pressure caused by the weight of a ship passing overhead.

Mines were destroyed by small, hard-working

Below Instructions are signalled to a minesweeping patrol off Britain's north-east coast, early on a March morning, 1940.

Below left How a minesweeper works to clear a minefield.

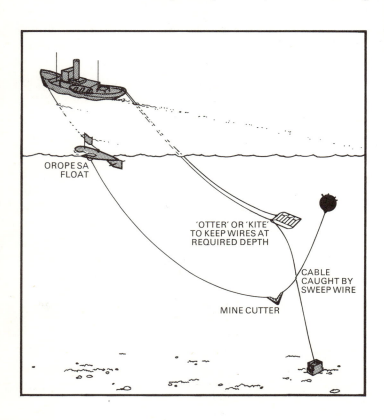

OROPESA FLOAT

'OTTER' OR 'KITE' TO KEEP WIRES AT REQUIRED DEPTH

CABLE CAUGHT BY SWEEP WIRE

MINE CUTTER

Above Lowering an Oropesa float during a minesweeping patrol.

vessels called minesweepers. There were fleet sweepers, specially-built shallow-draught ships; paddle minesweepers, adapted from peace time pleasure steamers; and converted trawlers. For the contact mine – the commonest of all – the minesweepers worked in pairs, each dragging a cigar-shaped sweep called the Oropesa at the end of a long wire. A device caused this wire to curve outwards in the water. When the wire met a mine's mooring wire, it cut it, and the buoyant mine popped to the surface. It would then be sunk by rifle fire.

The sweepers worked systematically up and down, like a lawnmower cutting grass. There were times, of course, when a sweeper would hit a mine itself. Some ships would be sunk outright while others struggled back to port with a huge gash in their side.

Magnetic mines were exploded by using special machinery which created a powerful magnetic effect; the acoustic by a type of road drill which made such a noise underwater that mines would explode a mile away. Pressure or "oyster" mines proved a failure – the Admiralty simply ordered ships to go slowly in shallow water where these mines were usually laid.

Life savers

Ships could be replaced, but experienced officers and seamen who drowned could not. At first, the hard-pressed escorts dared not stop to pick up survivors, for this would make them an easy target for U-boats. In time, new aids were introduced to help save lives. One way was the replacing of the old-fashioned cumbersome cork life-jacket with a softer buoyant waistcoat that could be worn at all times. Boats and emergency rafts were better equipped, too. They began to carry a machine for distilling fresh water from sea water, and a simple radio that automatically sent out distress signals. The lifeboat's white sails gave place to bright red ones, more easily seen from a distance. Smoke signals and distress rockets were also stowed away in the boats' lockers. Torpedoed seamen made incredible journeys in these boats. The record was held by a steward who was torpedoed in the Atlantic on 23rd November, 1942. Somehow he managed to survive for four and a half months – he was rescued off Brazil on 5th April, 1943. But many others died of exhaustion and exposure.

By 1941, most Atlantic convoys included a rescue ship. She would sail at the tail of the convoy – always a dangerous place – ready to rush to the scene of a sinking. As much of the rescue ship's work was done at night, she blatantly drew attention to herself by using searchlights to illumine men struggling in the water. She often had to sail between dozens of milling ships, in pitch darkness, which called for seamanship of the highest order.

These rescue ships were small vessels, rarely more than 1,500 tons. Each ship carried two huge baskets which were slung overboard, suspended from a derrick, with a seaman inside. As the ship moved slowly forward he literally fished the survivors out

Below Checking life-saving equipment was an important part of a ship's routine.

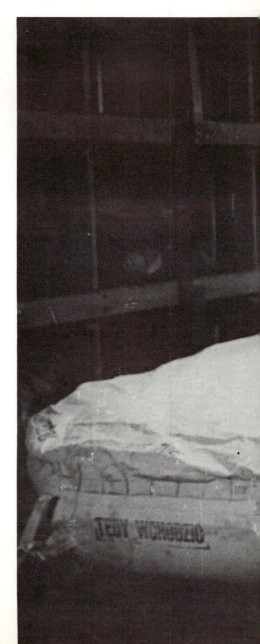

76

of the sea and into his basket. Large nets were also hung over the ship's side so that others, more active, could scramble up to the deck. Boats and rafts bobbed alongside and the survivors, half-dead from cold and shock, were hauled on board with bowlines about their waists.

A disastrous convoy battle

The winter of 1942–43 was hard. Gales and storms whipped the North Atlantic into a white fury. It became impossible to make observations from the pitching deck of a U-boat. Sinkings dropped and, although Doenitz had more than 160 boats on patrol, not one convoy was sighted. This was just as well, for the convoys were again desperately short of escorts. The invasion of French North Africa was under way, and most of the escort carriers were now needed in the Mediterranean. As the weather improved, so the Allied shipping losses mounted. In January it was 203,000 tons, in February 359,000, and by March 627,000 tons, a figure that recalled the bad days of the previous year. During March, 1943, the greatest convoy battle in history was fought.

Doenitz had news that two convoys, the slow SC-122 and the faster HX-229, were heading eastward. He had three packs in the area, totalling some forty U-boats, a formidable force. He sent them at once to await the arrival of the first convoy. This was the HX-229 – 38 ships with only four destroyers as escort. *U603* fired the first torpedo on the night of 16th March. Within minutes, one ship had been sunk and two more were stopped and listing. Three destroyers dashed to the rear to rescue survivors, leaving only one destroyer to look after the rest. By the time they returned, five more merchantmen had been sunk or crippled. The fight with HX-229 went on for another two nights. Then the slower SC-122, comprising 52 ships, was sighted some miles ahead. A pack of twelve U-boats surrounded it and, as the survivors of HX-229 loomed over the horizon, the two wolf packs joined forces and between them swamped the escorts.

By the time the two shattered convoys came within range of shore-based air cover, the battle had been

Above An Atlantic convoy rides at anchor in a British harbour after the dangerous crossing. In the foreground are the anti-aircraft guns of an escort ship.

raging for five days and five nights. Altogether 21 ships were lost, totalling 141,000 tons, and only one submarine, the *U384*, had been sunk. It was the most disastrous convoy battle ever known. If the sinkings went on at this rate, the Allies would lose not just the Battle of the Atlantic, but the war itself.

Turn of the tide

Flushed with success, Doenitz sent out more than a hundred U-boats to carry on the slaughter. But things did not work out as he had planned. A new aircraft, the long-range Liberator, came into operation from the end of March and, at the same time, the escort carriers returned from the Mediterranean. With them came a new threat, the M.A.C., or Merchant Aircraft Carrier, which carried more than a dozen fighter aircraft. As we have seen, these aircraft could land on the deck, refuel and take off again, and were much better equipped than the earlier Catapult carriers. The first of the M.A.C.s, the *Biter*, went into action at the end of March while escorting two convoys. Every time the U-Boats surfaced, they were dived on by fast fighter planes or the escort ships. The attack was finally called off when two U-boats were sunk – with not a single merchant ship taken. Much of this success was due to the new Commander-in-Chief of the Western Approaches, Admiral Sir Max Horton.

April, 1943, saw several desperate attacks on convoys, but the losses decreased rapidly. At the end

Gradually, the tide of battle turned in the Allies' favour. With the introduction of long-range flying boats *(top left)* and Merchant Aircraft Carriers, U-boats were sunk in increasing numbers *(bottom left)*.

of April, however, there was fierce battle between a pack of 51 U-boats and the outward bound convoy ONS-5, of 42 ships. The pack hit the convoy off Newfoundland; a violent storm forced it to break off the action, but during the night of 4th May it struck again. The merchantmen were silhouetted against the Northern Lights and seven were sunk before dawn. Next morning four of the damaged ships, struggling to keep up with the convoy, were also sent to the bottom. The morning of 6th May brought two anti-submarine support groups racing to the scene of battle, and four U-boats were sunk without further loss. The final score was twelve merchantmen and seven U-boats.

During May, June and July, more than ninety U-boats were destroyed. As Doenitz himself said later, it was the turning point in the Battle of the Atlantic. By the end of 1943, he had lost 237 submarines. And, although 3,600,000 tons of Allied shipping were destroyed, the Allied shipyards produced 14,500,000 tons of new merchant ships. This fantastic figure virtually replaced the entire Allied shipping losses for the first four years of the war.

The giant killers

In January, 1943, the battleship *Lützow* (formerly the *Deutschland*) and the heavy cruiser *Hipper*, were repulsed by a convoy's escort ships. Hitler was so furious that he sacked Grand Admiral Raeder in favour of Doenitz. Doenitz still believed that his submarines could win the war. By the end of the year it became obvious that his U-boats alone could not force the Allies to surrender. He now turned to his two giants, the *Tirpitz* and *Scharnhorst,* to see what they could do.

The *Scharnhorst* he sent north to attack a Russian-bound convoy protected by three cruisers, the *Belfast*, *Norfolk* and *Sheffield*, and some destroyers. The mighty battleship was sighted at daylight on 26th December, and there was a long-range gunnery duel during which she and the *Norfolk* were hit. Finally the *Scharnhorst* turned away for the Norwegian coast.

This news was picked up by a force pounding up from the south-west to intercept. It was led by one of Britain's biggest battleships, the *Duke of York*, in company with the cruiser *Jamaica* and four destroyers. As twilight fell, the shadowing cruisers sent up star-shells to mark the course of the battleship. One of these star-shells was spotted from the *Duke of York* and, next minute, to the surprise of the German Rear-Admiral Bey, 14-inch shells began to splash all around his ship. He returned fire, and although his ship was hit several times, it began to draw away from its enemy.

Fearing that the *Scharnhorst*'s speed would help her escape, Admiral Sir Bruce Fraser ordered his four destroyers into close-range attack. Soon the battleship was seen to be blazing furiously aft, and the *Jamaica* was sent in to finish her off. Struck by thirteen 14-inch shells, many 8-inch and 6-inch

Above On board the German battleship *Scharnhorst*. Notice the size of the guns.

shells and also by eleven torpedoes, the great *Scharnhorst* finally rolled over and sank. Only 36 of her 2,000 crew were saved.

The only capital ship left was the *Tirpitz*, still sheltering in a Norwegian fjord. On 12th November, 1944, twenty-nine Lancaster aircraft destroyed her with a salvo of 6-ton bombs. Both "giants" were now dead. The danger of attack by battleships on the convoys was finally gone.

U-boat killers

The anti-submarine support groups began operations at the end of 1942, but not until the spring of 1943 did they show their worth. Each group had its own aces, the most famous being Captain F. J. Walker. His Second Escort Group was so skilled and closely knit that it became a byword in the Atlantic.

At the end of January, 1944, Walker's ship the *Starling* was rolling and pitching in a seasonal Atlantic gale, together with the rest of the group –

Below The water heaves as a depth charge is dropped on an enemy U-boat.

Magpie, Woodpecker, Kite, Wild Goose and *Wren* — dangerous birds indeed! *Starling* was a typical escort sloop of 1,350 tons, and a speed of 20 knots. She carried six 4-inch and twelve 20 mm. anti-aircraft guns, and a crew of 192. The first contact with a U-boat was made on 31st January by *Wild Goose* which dropped a pattern of depth-charges. The submarine may have been surprised, for it crash-dived and turned away. This was what the escort sloops liked: to hunt at leisure while the convoy sailed on. Another attacking run by two of the sloops caused a great upheaval in the water. A large patch of oil and debris rose and fell with the swell. That was the end of *U592*.

The convoy steamed on, the long lines of merchant-men keeping station. The escorts wheeled ceaselessly up and down, waiting for the telltale "ping" of the asdic which revealed that a submarine was near. But there were no more reports until the night of 8th February. This time *U762* was picked up by the asdics and then, to the astonishment of the escorts, she suddenly surfaced. She came up so close to one of them that the sloop dared not use her depth charges or she would have blown off her own stern! But the *Woodpecker* came roaring up to drop her charges in a neat pattern above the disappearing U-boat. Once again oil and debris marked a kill.

Three hours later, during the morning of the 9th, *Starling* and *Wild Goose* destroyed *U734* in a similar fashion. Even as they were at work, *Kite* picked off another. After her deadly canisters had ripped the sea into tall columns of white water, *U238* joined the rest on the ocean floor. The final score was six U-boats in a passage of less than three weeks, a record for the Allies.

Victory and defeat

After the "Black May" of 1943, the U-boats were forced onto the defensive. Although Doenitz threw more of them into battle, more were being sunk than merchant ships. The reasons for this were fourfold: each convoy was now protected by (1) close surface escorts for defence, (2) anti-submarine support groups acting independently of the convoy, (3) escort carriers for detection and attack and (4) land-based bombers working with fighters from the escort carriers.

During October, 1944, Allied Coastal Command was allowed by Portugal to fly aircraft from the Azores, an invaluable mid-Atlantic base. Doenitz stated gloomily: "In the present phase of the campaign it is not victory, but the survival of boats and their crews that must take priority."

Doenitz was worried that so many U-boats were being sunk by attacking aircraft, so he armed his boats with more anti-aircraft guns. A few successes were scored, then the aircraft began to carry rockets. The U-boats had no defence against these.

A late-war invention was the *schnorkel*, a device consisting of a tube-within-a-tube. Fresh air could enter by one tube, while the other allowed the diesel fumes to escape. This meant that U-boats could stay submerged while recharging their batteries, leaving only the tip of the *schnorkel* to show above the surface. But even this clever device could not stop the continual sinking of U-boats. In any case, it had come too late.

At one minute past midnight on Tuesday, 8th May, 1945, Germany surrendered unconditionally to Great Britain, the United States and Russia. After five years and eight months, a "complete and crushing victory," as King George VI called it, had finally been won. By then, most of what was once the

Below The crew of a German U-boat shelter against the conning tower as their crippled vessel wallows in an angry sea.

proud and powerful German navy had been destroyed. Only three cruisers, the *Prinz Eugen, Nürnberg* and *Leipzig*, a few destroyers and some 400 U-boats remained to surrender. The Battle of the Atlantic was over.

The U-boat hunters

DESTROYERS The backbone of convoy defence. Their size varied between 900 (Hunt Class) and 1,900 tons ("L" Class). Speed about 36 knots. Armament four 7-inch guns, A.A. guns and four to eight torpedo tubes.

CORVETTES These were found rather small for mid-ocean work. 925 tons, one 4-inch and one multiple pom-pom gun.

FRIGATES Excellent all-round anti-submarine ships. 1,370 tons, 20 knots, two 4-inch, ten 20 mm. A.A. guns.

SUNDERLAND Flying Boats. 2,980 miles range. Two .50-inch and up to twelve .303-inch machine guns. Carried bombs or depth charges.

WELLINGTON A stalwart Coastal Command bomber. 3,200 mile range. Four .303 machine guns and bombs.

CATALINA American-designed flying boat. 3,750 mile range. Six .303-inch machine guns, four depth charges.

Table of dates

1939

1st September	Germany invades Poland.
3rd September	Britain declares war on Germany.
4th September	Liner *Athenia* torpedoed off Ireland.
17th September	Aircraft carrier *Courageous* sunk.
13th October	Battleship *Royal Oak* sunk at Scapa Flow by Prien in *U47*.
8th November	Germans begin using magnetic mines.
23rd November	*Rawalpindi* sunk by the *Scharnhorst* and *Gneisenau*.
13th December	Battle of the River Plate.
18th December	The *Graf Spee* scuttles at the entrance to Montevideo harbour.

1940

January	"De-gaussing" applied to Allied ships to combat menace of magnetic mines.
24th May	British army is evacuated from Dunkirk.
3rd September	Anglo-American "lease-lend" agreement signed – British bases are traded for fifty U.S. destroyers.
5th November	German pocket battleship *Admiral Scheer* sinks the *Jervis Bay*.

1941

18th May	German warships *Bismarck* and *Prinz Eugen* sail for the Atlantic.
24th May	H.M.S. *Hood* sunk.
27th May	*Bismarck* sunk.
1st June	*Prinz Eugen* returns to Brest.
22nd June	Germany attacks Russia. First Allied convoy with surface escorts all the way crosses the Atlantic.
6th December	Japanese attack Pearl Harbor.
11th December	The second U-boat victory phase begins with a mass sinking of ships off the American coast.

1942
27th March   Raid on St. Nazaire (Operation "Chariot").
July   U-boats concentrated in the North Atlantic.
September   The first anti-submarine support group begins operations.
November   The worst month for sinkings by U-boats. 118 ships totalling 743,321 tons are sunk.

1943
16th–20th March   Largest convoy battle in history. HX-229 and SC-122 lose 21 ships for the loss of one U-boat.
May   165,000 tons of shipping lost at a cost of 40 U-boats.
June   17 U-boats are sunk for only 18,000 tons of merchant shipping.
22nd September   *Tirpitz* severely damaged by British midget submarines.
26th December   *Scharnhorst* sunk in a battle off North Cape.
28th December   Three German destroyers sunk and several damaged by British cruisers in the Bay of Biscay.

1944
3rd April   *Tirpitz* damaged by carrier planes.
6th June   France invaded by Allied forces (D-day).
15th September   *Tirpitz* further crippled by heavy bombers.
12th November   *Tirpitz* finally sunk by heavy bombers.

1945
30th April   Hitler commits suicide in Berlin.
9th May   Victory in Europe (VE-day) celebrated.
14th August   Japan surrenders to the Allies.
2nd September   End of World War Two.

Glossary

AFT At or near the stern (or back) of a ship.

ASDIC A sonor device for detecting submerged submarines. It was originally produced by the Allied Submarine Detection Investigation Committee, hence its name.

ATLANTIC CHARTER An agreement of mutual support pledged by Winston Churchill and President Roosevelt in August, 1941.

BINNACLE Container for a ship's compass.

BLACK GAP The middle of the Atlantic through which the convoys had to pass without surface or air protection.

C.A.M. Catapult Aircraft Merchantmen – merchant ships equipped with catapults which could launch fighter aircraft when the convoy was threatened by an enemy bomber.

COMMODORE The senior officer in charge of a convoy.

CONVOY A number of merchant ships sailing together with an armed escort.

DEPTH CHARGE A cannister containing a high explosive, which could be made to explode at a pre-determined depth.

DERRICK A crane with a movable arm.

ESCORT CARRIERS Merchant ships converted to carry aircraft. They were used mainly to close the Black Gap.

FLYING BOAT An aircraft with a boat-like hull which enabled it to take off and land on water.

HYDROPHONE A listening device used by submarines to relay the sound of propellers from above.

M.A.C. Merchant Aircraft Carrier – a merchant ship with a flight deck built on her so that fighter aircraft could take off and land.

MINE A container filled with high explosive which was placed in the sea, and would explode when a ship passed overhead.

MINESWEEPERS Small trawler-like vessels used to find and destroy mines.

PERISCOPE A long tube-like instrument which allows someone in a submarine to view the surface. It works through an arrangement of prisms or mirrors.

POCKET BATTLESHIP A German warship of only 10,000 tons but which was armed with weapons of much larger vessels. The most famous was the *Graf Spee*.

RADAR A system for judging the direction and distance of an object by measuring the radio waves which it reflects.

SCHNORKEL A device used by U-boats which enabled them to take in fresh air, and expel foul air, while still submerged.

TANKER A ship designed to carry a liquid cargo, especially oil.

TORPEDO A long cigar-shaped weapon, tipped with a war-head containing high explosive, which is fired from submarines and surface vessels.

TRAMP A cargo-carrying ship which, in peacetime, wandered from port to port picking up what cargoes she could.

U-BOAT A German submarine, from the German word *Unterseeboot* (under-sea-boat). Each U-boat was known by a number, e.g. *U54, U801* . . .

WESTERN APPROACHES The western Atlantic, and the sea around the west coast of Great Britain.

WOLF PACK A system whereby U-boats massed together to attack a convoy and its escorts.

WRENS Members of the Women's Royal Naval Service (or W.R.N.S.)

Further Reading

Berthold, W., *The Sinking of the Bismarck* (Longmans, 1958) – the cat-and-mouse hunt by the Royal Navy for the German battleship *Bismarck,* and the drama of their final success.

Dupuy, T. N., *The Naval War in the West – Vol. 4 The Raiders, Vol. 5 The Wolf Packs* (Ward, 1964) – a clear, well-illustrated account of Britain's struggle to keep her ships afloat in the face of superior German air and sea power.

Gibson, C., *The Ship with Five Names* (Abelard-Schuman, 1965) – the adventures of a British tramp-ship captured by the Germans and converted into a minelayer.

Monsarrat, N., *The Cruel Sea* (Cassell, 1966) – an exciting story describing the exploits of a corvette and her crew during World War Two.

Stafford, E. P., *The Far and the Deep* (Arthur Barker, 1968) – a comprehensive history of the development of submarines. There is a good section explaining their importance in World War Two. Best for older readers.

Waldron, T. J. & Gleeson, J., *The Frogmen* (Evans, 1966) – some of the most dangerous exploits of World War Two were the raids against enemy docks and harbours carried out by frogmen, who planted deadly underwater bombs.

Woodrooffe, T., *The Battle of the Atlantic* (Faber, 1965) – the author traces in a clear and straight-forward manner the course of the Battle of the Atlantic, and explains how it affected the outcome of World War Two on other fronts.

Index

Picture Credits

The author and Publishers wish to thank all those who gave permission for the reproduction of copyright photographs on the following pages: Conway Picture Library, 34, 70–71; Paul Popper, 23; Radio Times Hulton Picture Library, *frontispiece*, *jacket* (back), 9, 10–11, 16–17, 20–21, 29, 30–31 (bottom), 32–33, 35, 41, 43, 47, 49, 52, 58–59, 62, 66–67, 68–69, 72–73, 74, 75, 76–77, 80–81, 84–85; Keystone Picture Agency, 13, 19, 24–25, 26–27, 28–29, 30–31 (top), 36, 37, 38–39, 44–45, 51, 55, 57, 60–61, 64, 65, 78, 79, 80, 82–83, 87, 88 (bottom), 89; Fox Photos, 88 (*top* and *centre*), the Trustees of the late Norman Wilkinson, *jacket* (front).
The drawings and diagrams were done by Grout, Fry and Associates.